SPACE

From the solar system to black holes,
explore the secrets of the universe

Contents

LITTLE TIGER
LONDON

CATERPILLAR BOOKS
An imprint of the Little Tiger Group
www.littletiger.co.uk
1 Coda Studios, 189 Munster Road, London SW6 6AW
Imported into the EEA by Penguin Random House Ireland,
Morrison Chambers, 32 Nassau Street, Dublin DO2 YH68
First published in Great Britain 2022
Text by Noodle Fuel 2022
Illustrations by Rich Watson 2022
Copyright © NOODLE FUEL Ltd 2022
All rights reserved • Printed in China
A CIP catalogue record of this book is available from the British Library
ISBN: 978-1-83891-457-8 • CPB/2800/2079/1121
10 9 8 7 6 5 4 3 2 1

The Forest Stewardship Council® (FSC®) is an international, non-governmental organisation dedicated to promoting responsible management of the world's forests. FSC operates a system of forest certification and product labelling that allows consumers to identify wood and wood-based products from well-managed forests.

FSC
www.fsc.org
MIX
Paper from
responsible sources
FSC® C017606

For more information about the FSC,
please visit their website at www.fsc.org.

This symbol means that we're dealing with a very big number indeed!

Where you see this symbol, you can be sure that this is a record-breaking fact!

And these facts will absolutely burst your brain!

The universe is weird – really, REALLY weird.

We're going to show you that the universe is a **very strange but completely fascinating place**, and that the only thing that's more interesting is the people who want to go and explore it! So come with us and let's **journey deep into...**

SPACE

Most people believe that the universe formed about **13.8 billion years ago** in a process called the Big Bang.

This was much more successful than the Little Bang, which everyone agreed was a bit of a let-down.

There are billions, possibly **trillions**, of galaxies in the **universe**.

very **BIG** *number*

A galaxy is a huge collection of gas, dust and billions of stars and their solar systems.

You may not be feeling small yet, but give us a minute...

Our galaxy is called the Milky Way. It takes **230 million years** for the Sun (and our solar system) to orbit its centre.

COME ON! YOU GOTTA WORK ON THOSE LAP TIMES!

It would take more than a million years for a high-speed jet to reach our **nearest star** after the Sun, Proxima Centauri.

LADIES AND GENTLEMEN, I'M AFRAID WE'VE RUN OUT OF PEANUTS.

The Solar System

A **planetary system** is a set of objects, such as planets or asteroids, that orbit a star. There are over 2,500 such systems in our galaxy. We call our planetary system – the Sun and the objects that orbit it – the **solar system**.

It takes Earth about **365 days** to orbit the Sun. This is our year. Earth makes a full rotation on its axis in **24 hours**. This is our day.

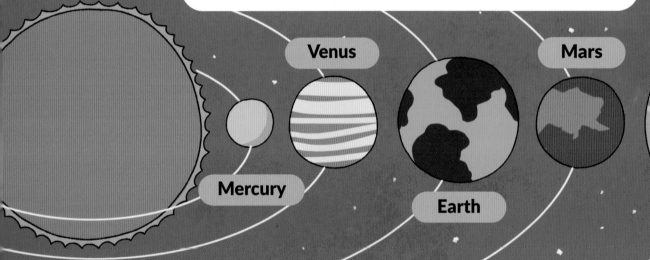

Mercury

Venus

Earth

Mars

Jupiter

The solar system was formed around **4.5 billion years** ago.

COME ON NOW EVERYONE, NICE NEAT ORBITS!

Until 16th century astronomer **Nicolaus Copernicus** showed us that the planets orbit the Sun, people believed that Earth was the centre of the solar system.

IT'S NOT ALL ABOUT YOU! YOU'RE SO SELF-CENTRED!

The Sun alone makes up over **99%** of the mass (amount of matter) in the solar system.

★ BRAIN ★ BURSTER

Saturn

Neptune

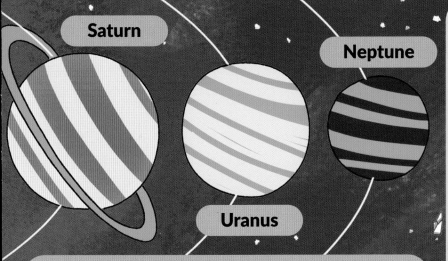

Uranus

Beyond the main planets is the **Kuiper belt** – a region full of icy objects, such as Pluto.

I USED TO BE A PLANET, YOU KNOW.

Pluto was considered a planet until 2006.

Interstellar space is the area beyond the edge of the Sun's magnetic field.

Voyager 1 was the first spacecraft to reach interstellar space and it took **35 years** to get there from Earth!

ARE WE THERE YET?

The distance from the Sun to Neptune, the furthest planet, is over **4,500,000,000km** (2,800,000,000mi)!

very **BIG** number

The Planets

Mercury is the closest planet to the Sun and is **extremely hot**!

Temperatures there can reach **430°C** (800°F) on its surface!

Make sure to bring some factor one million sun cream if you visit!

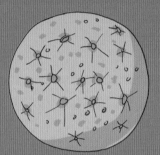

Venus has **no moons** and may have been much more like Earth a long time ago!

It's a bit different now though. Venus is the **hottest planet** and the temperatures on the surface are scorching enough to melt metal!

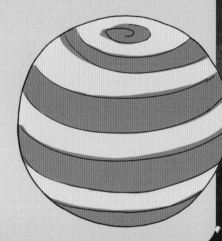

Earth is the fifth largest planet. About **70%** of its surface is covered in water. Earth is the only planet known to support life.

Scientists are searching for **signs of life** on other planets, such as Mars.

OF COURSE, WE MIGHT FIND YOU FIRST!

Mars has massive dust storms that can **last for weeks** and cover half the planet!

THE WORST PART IS THE HOOVERING AFTERWARDS!

Jupiter is the biggest planet – you could fit more than **1,300 Earths** inside it!

RECORD BREAKER

Don't mention the big red spot though, Jupiter is very sensitive about it!

Saturn is famous for its **beautiful rings** made of ice, rocks and dust.

The other planets gave up waiting for a turn with the hula-hoop ages ago!

Neptune is the coldest planet. Temperatures there can reach as low as **-240°C** (-400°F)!

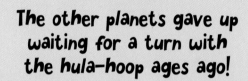

You would certainly need a coat...

Uranus is tilted on its **side**.

Or is Uranus straight and all the other planets are tilted?

★ BRAIN ★ BURSTER

Scientists think there might be an undiscovered **Planet X** somewhere beyond the icy Kuiper belt. We can't see it because it's so far away, but scientists are working on ways to detect it!

Stars

There are more than **100,000,000,000** stars in the Milky Way galaxy.

It took a long time to count them.

21, 22, 23, 24, 25...

very **BIG** number

The Sun's light takes just over **eight minutes** to reach us, but the light from the next closest star takes over **four years** to get here!

So the Sun in the sky isn't what the Sun looks like right now, but what it looked like **eight minutes ago**!

You may think the Sun is big and bright, but the **Pistol Star** has 100 times more mass and is **ten million times** brighter.

YEEHAW!

The **closest star** to the Earth is our Sun.

LOVE YOU, MUM!

Stars shine through a process called **fusion**. Inside a star, hydrogen is converted into **helium**, releasing huge amounts of light.

Fusion is being researched as a future power source here on Earth.

How stars are formed...

1

Gravity disturbances cause gas and dust in space to start to clump together.

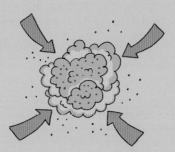

2

As it gets bigger, the clump of gas and dust begins to rotate and flattens out.

3

The disc starts to spin faster and faster, attracting more matter and forming a hot centre called a protostar.

4

Hydrogen atoms in the protostar begin to fuse together, producing huge amounts of energy. Finally, a star is born!

Blue stars are the **hottest** and red stars are the **coolest**.

Just like your kitchen taps... No, wait! Hang on a minute!

WE JUST LIKE TO MAKE SURE THAT YOU'RE PAYING ATTENTION!

When large stars reach the end of their lives, they **explode** into spectacular supernovas.

A **galaxy** is a system of millions or even billions of stars clustered together. Our solar system is in the **Milky Way** galaxy and makes up just a tiny part of it.

Constellations

A constellation is a **group of stars** that resembles an object or pattern. Constellations are often named after **mythical creatures** or objects.

Your location on the planet and the **time of year** affect what constellations you can see in the sky.

It also has to be night-time, but we're hoping you'd figured that one out for yourself.

In ancient times, constellations were used to keep track of the **calendar**. This was vital information for farmers planting and harvesting crops.

The largest constellation, **Hydra**, takes up around 3% of the sky. The smallest, **Crux**, only takes up 0.17%.

The Greek mathematician **Ptolemy** listed 48 ancient constellations. Modern astronomers have added another 40 constellations, bringing the grand total to 88!

WHAT MONTH IS IT?

I'LL TELL YOU TONIGHT...

Constellations were **essential for navigation** before modern satellite mapping systems.

YOU HAVE REACHED YOUR DESTINATION...

The word 'constellation' comes from a Latin phrase meaning **set with stars**.

Leo is named after the mythical Nemean lion whose skin could not be cut by weapons. The **hero Heracles** fought the lion and killed it with his bare hands.

I'M THE MANE MAN!

In Greek mythology, **Scorpius** was a scorpion that stung the great hunter Orion to death. The constellation of Scorpius is home to some of the **brightest stars** in the night sky.

The gigantic crab, **Cancer**, was sent by the goddess Hera to attack Hercules as he fought the monstrous Hydra. Hercules made short work of the **giant-clawed beast**, crushing it with his foot!

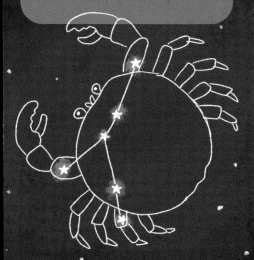

When Zeus fell in love with the Princess Europa, he transformed himself into a white bull with golden horns named **Taurus** and carried her away to Crete.

Because nothing says "I love you" better than... erm... transforming into a bull.

IT WAS EITHER THAT OR A LABRADOR PUPPY.

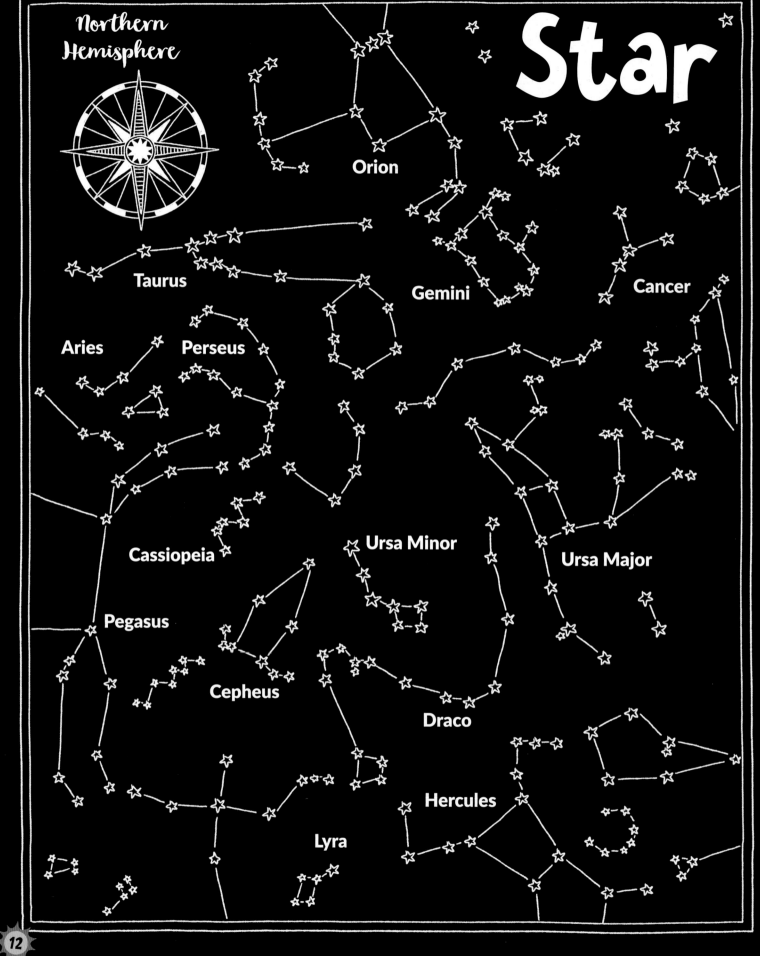

Northern Hemisphere

Star

Orion

Taurus

Gemini

Cancer

Aries

Perseus

Cassiopeia

Ursa Minor

Ursa Major

Pegasus

Cepheus

Draco

Hercules

Lyra

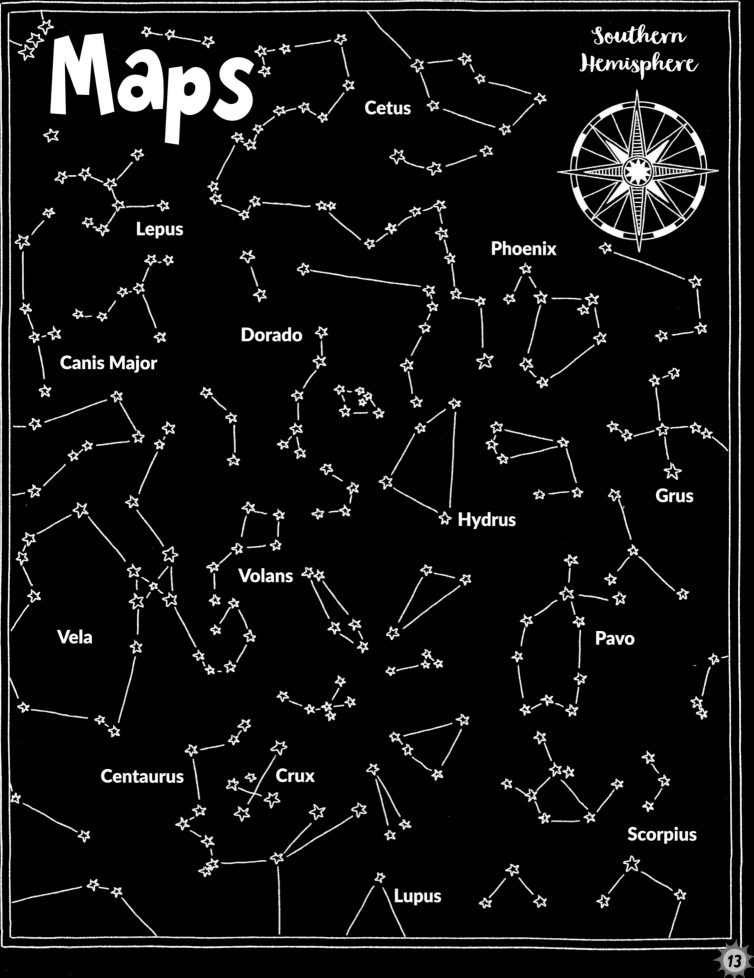

The Moon

Most planets are **orbited** by moons. Earth has only one – the Moon!

Saturn, on the other hand, has 82 moons, which frankly just seems greedy!

Gravity – the **invisible force** that pulls things together – keeps the planets in orbit around the Sun, and the Moon in orbit around Earth.

On average, the Moon is **384,400km** (238,855mi) from Earth and it completes a full orbit every 27 days.

As the **strength of gravity** on the Moon is about **one-sixth** of that on Earth, you would only weigh a sixth of your normal weight there.

WHEEEEEE!

The phases of the Moon

Sometimes you will see a **full Moon**, other times a half Moon or crescent. It depends which part of the Moon is being lit up by the Sun. These **sunlit areas** are called 'phases' of the Moon.

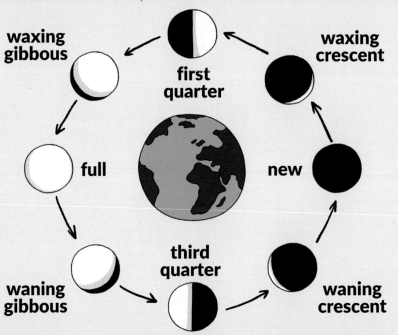

waxing gibbous

waxing crescent

first quarter

full

new

waning gibbous

third quarter

waning crescent

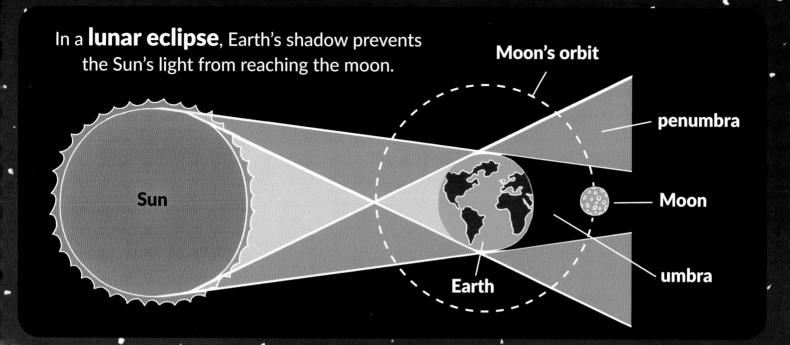

In a **lunar eclipse**, Earth's shadow prevents the Sun's light from reaching the moon.

Moon's orbit

Sun

penumbra

Moon

umbra

Earth

The **gravitational pull** of the Moon on Earth's water causes waves and tides.

SURF'S UP, DUDES!

The temperature on the Moon ranges from -130°C (-200°F) to 120°C (250°F), depending on the **amount of sunlight** hitting the surface.

THERE'S A REASON OUR SUITS ARE AIR-CONDITIONED!

The Moon is about a quarter of the size of Earth, but Earth weighs almost **80 times** more.

I'VE ALREADY TOLD YOU THAT'S NOT BECAUSE IT'S MADE OF CHEESE.

RECORD BREAKER

The bumps you can see on the Moon are **giant craters**. The biggest is the South Pole-Aitken basin which is about 2,560km (1,600mi) across and 8km (5mi) deep!

Space Travel

In the 20th century, the USA and USSR competed in a **space race**. Both nations tried to be the first to send a person to space.

The USSR got there first when the cosmonaut **Yuri Gagarin** orbited Earth in 1961.

Unmanned probes have now been sent to every planet in the solar system, as well as to comets and asteroids.

ARE THE HUMANS EVER GOING TO GET HERE?

The first animals to be intentionally sent into space were **fruit flies**. They were put on board a rocket launched in 1947!

THE NAME'S ALDRIN... BUZZ ALDRIN!

Since it was launched in 1977, **Voyager 1** has travelled over 23,000,000,000km (14,000,000,000mi) – further than any other spacecraft. It was the first human-made object to leave our solar system.

RECORD BREAKER

You can grow a **few centimetres taller** in space because there is less gravity pushing you down.

The **International Space Station** (ISS), located in Earth's orbit, has been occupied since 2000 and people from lots of different countries have worked there.

Instead of sending humans to Mars, robotic vehicles called **Mars Rovers** have been used to examine the planet.

We hope to go there ourselves soon!

The first **tourist** to pay to travel to space was American millionaire Dennis Tito in 2001.

In 1969, Buzz Aldrin and Neil Armstrong, aboard the Apollo 11 spacecraft, were the first people to land on the Moon. It took them about four days to get there. The last Moon landing was in 1972, but there are plans for humans to return there soon!

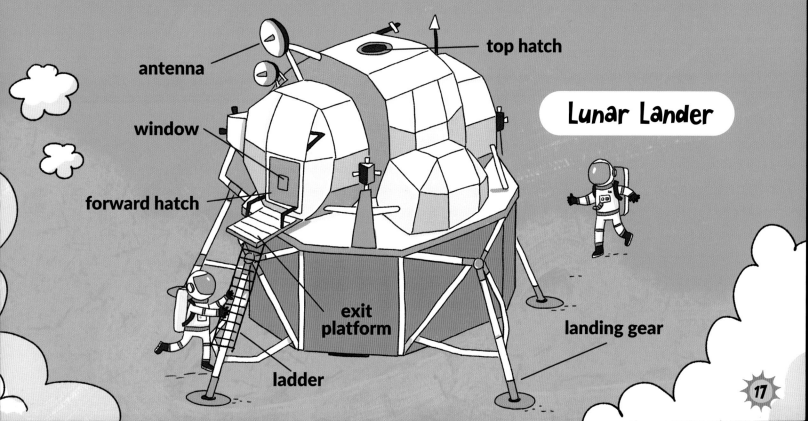

antenna

top hatch

window

Lunar Lander

forward hatch

exit platform

landing gear

ladder

Astronauts

Astronauts live and work on the **International Space Station**. They travel there by rocket or shuttle.

Because it's much, much quicker than walking.

The word 'astronaut' comes from the Greek *astron nautes*, which means **star sailor**.

MOOOON RIIIIVER!

On the ISS, astronauts have to strap themselves to a **special space toilet**, when doing their business, to make sure they don't float away.

There's nothing funny about a floater on the space station!

Most astronauts are **scientists** who have trained for several years. They also need to be able to swim, speak Russian and pilot a jet plane.

Not all at the same time, though!

'Cosmonaut' is the **Russian** word for astronaut.

NO, 'ASTRONAUT' IS THE ENGLISH WORD FOR COSMONAUT!

H_2... OH!

Astronauts drink **recycled** water.

And yes, that does mean what you think it means...

The American space organisation NASA has a special aircraft that trains astronauts in what it feels like to be **weightless**. It can make some people feel sick!

This has earned the plane the nickname the 'Vomit Comet'.

I HATE TUESDAYS...

In 1971, Apollo 14 astronaut Alan Shepard was the first person **to play golf** on the Moon.

WHY DO YOU ALWAYS BRING A SPARE SPACESUIT?

IN CASE I GET A HOLE IN ONE...

Readjusting to **gravity** can be a problem for astronauts returning home. It can make each step on Earth feel **very heavy**.

SHE'S BEEN LIKE THIS EVER SINCE SHE GOT HOME!

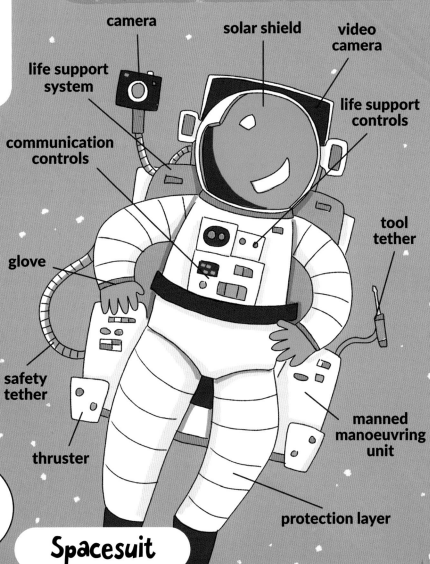

camera

life support system

solar shield

video camera

life support controls

communication controls

glove

tool tether

safety tether

thruster

manned manoeuvring unit

protection layer

Spacesuit

A DAY in the Life of an ASTRONAUT

OCCASIONALLY, WE GET TO GO FOR A SPACEWALK OUTSIDE — A DEFINITE HIGHLIGHT.

WE WORK HARD EVERY DAY ON SCIENTIFIC EXPERIMENTS OR REPAIRS.

WE RELAX AT THE END OF THE DAY. WE CAN WATCH FILMS AND TV, BUT THE BEST THING TO LOOK AT IS THE VIEW.

WE HAVE TO EXERCISE EACH DAY AS WEIGHTLESSNESS MEANS OUR MUSCLES AND BONES WEAKEN OVER TIME.

AND THEN WE'RE BACK TO WHERE WE STARTED — AND DO IT ALL OVER AGAIN THE NEXT DAY.

Satellites

Artificial satellites – **machines that orbit Earth** – are used for communication (for example, to relay TV signals and phone calls), mapping and monitoring the weather.

They also give scientists an excuse to launch rockets and, let's face it, rockets are cool!

The first satellite, **Sputnik 1**, was launched in 1957. It was about the size of a beach ball and took 98 minutes to orbit Earth.

The Russian scientist **Konstantin Tsiolkovsky** first suggested the idea of launching humans into orbit in 1903!

Satellites are sent into space on top of **rockets**.

Geostationary satellites orbit the equator at the **same speed** as Earth's rotation, so from the ground they don't seem to move.

Satellites travel around the world at a speed of **27,300kmph** (17,000mph) or more.

very **BIG** number

As more satellites are launched, the chances of a **crash** increase. In 2009, two communications satellites collided in space.

Secret spy photos taken by early satellites were dropped from space in a canister and scooped up by planes in mid-air!

★ BRAIN BURSTER

Overgrown ancient **Mayan ruins** were found in the middle of a jungle in Mexico by mapping satellites.

More than 20 satellites make up the **Global Positioning System**, or GPS, which can tell your precise location anywhere on Earth.

The International Space Station is the **largest artificial satellite** currently orbiting Earth.

Space Junk

Of the **5,000 artificial satellites** in orbit, only around 2,500 are operational. The others have now become space junk!

Space junk is all the rubbish left in space by humans. The weight of all the debris in orbit is thought to be around **8,800 tonnes** (9,700 tons).

That would fill 600 dustbin lorries!

Some **weird things** have become space junk. These include a glove, a tool bag, pliers, a camera and... erm... a spatula.

A SPATULA?

As of 2020, **34,000 large pieces** of space junk are in orbit, but there are also many smaller bits that are too tiny to track.

very BIG number

The International Space Station is sometimes forced to manoeuvre out of the way to avoid a **collision** with space junk!

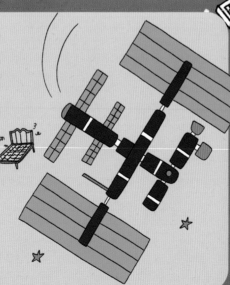

Every year, between 200–400 pieces of tracked junk **burn up** when re-entering Earth's atmosphere.

Shooting star just sounds better than blazing ball of rubbish!

If space junk is not cleared away, it could make space travel too **dangerous**, trapping us on Earth!

1957

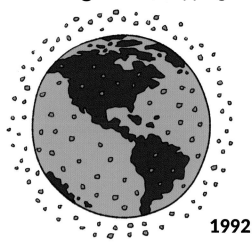
1992

2015

In 2018, a net designed to catch junk in orbit and **burn it** in the atmosphere was successfully tested for the first time.

WELL, I WASN'T EXPECTING AN OCTOPUS...

The chance of you getting hit by a falling piece of space junk is **ten million** times smaller than the odds of being struck by lightning.

THAT'S REASSURING!

★ BRAIN BURSTER

A piece of **space debris** can reach speeds of up to 8kmps (5mps). That's nearly seven times faster than a bullet!

Astronauts may be put in **danger** by space junk because their spacesuits can't protect them from the debris.

In 2007, China **deliberately destroyed** one of its weather satellites to test a new weapon. That test created over 3,000 pieces of space debris.

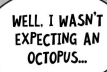

Asteroids, Comets and Space

Space is completely **silent**. Sound can't travel through a vacuum (a space with little or no matter).

There is no air in space, which is why astronauts need **oxygen supplies** in their spacesuits.

We're not sure why they need the chocolate biscuit dispenser...

IS THE ASTRONAUT CHOIR ANY GOOD?

I HAVE NO IDEA!

Space is not **truly empty**, there are traces of gas and dust particles, but they are spread over vast distances.

WELL, I DO LIKE TO KEEP THE PLACE LOOKING NICE!

The temperature can fall to **-270°C** (-458°F) in the **void** of space.

Space begins 100km (62mi) above the surface of Earth.

This means the average person could walk there in three days. The path's quite steep though!

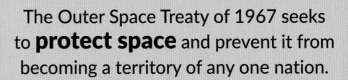

The Outer Space Treaty of 1967 seeks to **protect space** and prevent it from becoming a territory of any one nation.

Comets are lumps of ice and dust that orbit the Sun. They have **long tails** that are formed by ice and dust evaporating due to the Sun's heat.

The most famous comet is **Halley's Comet**. It orbits the Sun every 75 years and will next be visible from Earth in 2061.

Asteroids are large rocky bodies that orbit the Sun. The majority are found in the **asteroid belt** between Mars and Jupiter.

The asteroid belt was formed after the asteroid trousers became too loose around the waist.

Asteroids can vary between 1.8m (6ft) and 965km (600mi) in diameter. A collision with a **large asteroid** would be very dangerous for life on Earth.

Just ask the dinosaurs!

Meteors are lumps of rock or dust particles that **burn up** as they enter Earth's atmosphere, leaving fiery trails in the sky.

Or it might just be a spatula burning up on re-entry.

Meteors that do not burn up but hit the ground are called **meteorites** and are **highly prized** by collectors.

Black Holes

Black holes are formed when massive stars (much bigger than the Sun) die. The **dying star** collapses in on itself, forming an area of extremely intense gravity.

The closest black hole to Earth that we know of is about 1,000 light years away. A light year is **9.5 trillion km** (6 trillion mi).

very **BIG** number

Which is quite close enough, thank you!

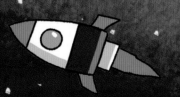

A black hole's gravity is **so strong** that it consumes everything around it, even light. This means that black holes are invisible.

Objects that are drawn into a black hole are stretched by the effects of gravity. This process is called **spaghettification**!

Once it starts to happen, you're pasta point of no return!

Sagittarius A* is a black hole at the centre of our own galaxy, the Milky Way. It has a mass over four million times greater than that of the Sun.

So our galaxy is really just swirling around a giant plug hole!

The famous German-born physicist **Albert Einstein** suggested that black holes existed way back in 1915. It was over fifty years before one was actually found, finally proving his theory to be correct.

Red Dwarfs and Other Stars

A red dwarf is a star that is small and cool – **cooler** than our Sun.

WHY ARE YOU WEARING SUNGLASSES INDOORS?

You can't see red dwarfs in the night sky with your **naked eye** because they burn much more dimly than other stars.

Red dwarfs are the most common type of star in our galaxy, making up about **75%** of the stars.

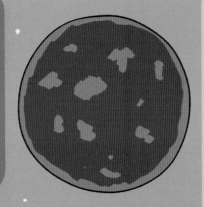

Red dwarfs have much **longer lifespans** than other types of star. They can live for up to ten trillion years.

I REMEMBER THE BIG BANG LIKE IT WAS JUST YESTERDAY.

Neutron stars are the crushed remains of big stars that have **exploded** as supernovas.

I THINK I OVERDID IT THIS MORNING!

Neutron stars are very small, only about 20km (12mi) in diameter, but they are very heavy. A piece of neutron star the size of a matchbox would weigh more than **Mount Everest**!

★ BRAIN ★ BURSTER

Pulsars are a type of **fast-spinning** neutron star that shoot out enormous beams of light and radiation (high-energy waves). They were discovered by Jocelyn Bell Burnell in 1967.

Pulsars spin incredibly fast, up to **700 revolutions per second**. If you were standing on a pulsar, you would be travelling at a quarter of the speed of light!

Hope you don't get dizzy!

When pulsars were first detected, scientists weren't sure what they were. They even thought that they might be **alien transmissions**. This earned pulsars the nickname 'LGM', short for 'Little Green Men'!

WHO ARE YOU CALLING 'LITTLE'?

★ BRAIN ★ BURSTER

Magnetars are neutron stars with **very powerful magnetic fields**.

An explosion on a magnetar called **SGR 1806-20** released more energy in a tenth of a second than the Sun has produced in the last 100,000 years.

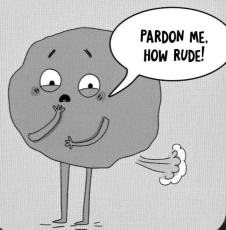

PARDON ME, HOW RUDE!

The huge magnetic field of a magnetar star is so powerful that the surface of the star regularly **collapses and explodes**.

Mars Mission

The planet Mars is just over **half** the size of Earth.

Mars is known as the **red planet** and is named after the Roman god of war.

Not a chocolate bar.

The first human-made object to successfully land on Mars was the **Mars 3 space probe**, launched by the USSR in 1971.

Mars was once much more similar to Earth, with **liquid water** and a thick atmosphere.

OH, MARS USED TO BE FUN, DARLING, BUT NOW THERE'S JUST NO ATMOSPHERE.

The surface of Mars is a **hostile environment**, unsuitable for human survival. Its atmosphere has no ozone layer to protect lifeforms from the Sun's radiation, and it lacks surface water.

Curiosity is a car-sized robotic rover designed to explore Mars. It was launched from Cape Canaveral, USA, on 26ᵗʰ November 2011 and landed on Mars on 6ᵗʰ August 2012.

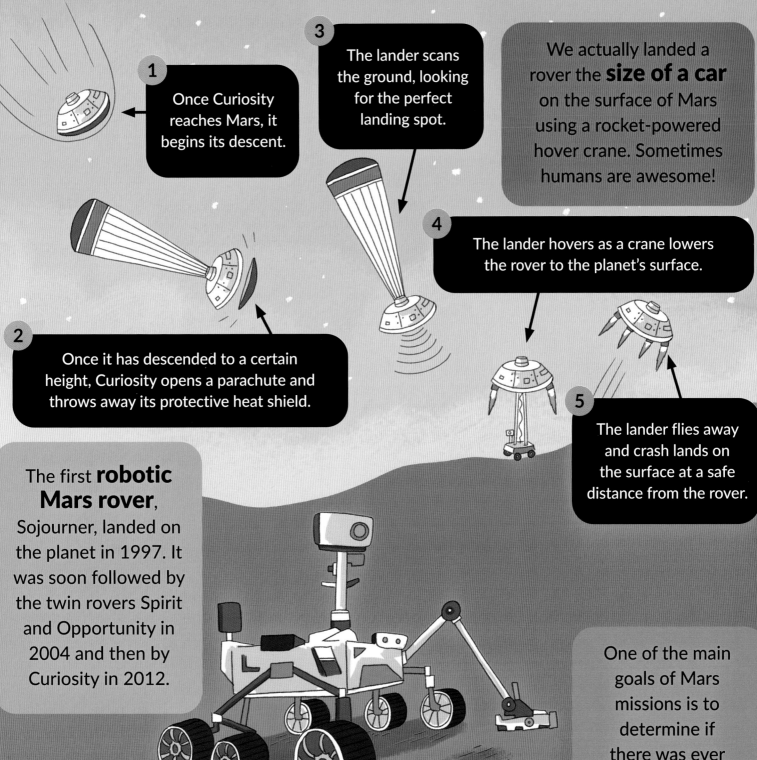

1 Once Curiosity reaches Mars, it begins its descent.

2 Once it has descended to a certain height, Curiosity opens a parachute and throws away its protective heat shield.

3 The lander scans the ground, looking for the perfect landing spot.

4 The lander hovers as a crane lowers the rover to the planet's surface.

5 The lander flies away and crash lands on the surface at a safe distance from the rover.

We actually landed a rover the **size of a car** on the surface of Mars using a rocket-powered hover crane. Sometimes humans are awesome!

The first **robotic Mars rover**, Sojourner, landed on the planet in 1997. It was soon followed by the twin rovers Spirit and Opportunity in 2004 and then by Curiosity in 2012.

One of the main goals of Mars missions is to determine if there was ever **life on Mars**.

Space Timeline

13.8 billion years ago
The Universe forms in an event called the **Big Bang**.

4.5 billion years ago
Our **solar system** forms.

RIGHT, CAN ANYONE PLAY DRUMS?

Circa 2000BCE
The Sumerians make the first records of **constellations**.

1543
Nicolaus Copernicus publishes his theory that planets **orbit** the Sun.

1781
Uranus is the first planet to be discovered that can't be seen with the naked eye.

1846
Neptune is discovered.

FOUND YOU!

4ᵗʰ October 1957
The first satellite, **Sputnik 1**, (USSR) is launched.

3ʳᵈ November 1957
Sputnik 2 is launched by the USSR with a dog called **Laika** on board.

12th April 1961

Yuri Gagarin is the **first person** in space.

Frogs, tortoises, dogs, monkeys, pigs and fruit flies got there before him!

1st October 1958
NASA is formed.

16th June 1963

Cosmonaut Valentina Tereshkova is the **first woman** in space.

18th October 1965
The **first spacewalk** is performed by cosmonaut Alexei Leonov.

3rd February 1966
The first controlled **moon landing** is made by Luna 9 (USSR).

20th July 1969
American astronaut Neil Armstrong is the first person to **walk on the Moon**, during the Apollo 11 mission.

20th November 1998
The first part of the **International Space Station** is launched.

30th May 2020

SpaceX becomes the first **private company** to send astronauts to the ISS. In October, the ISS also receives a brand-new toilet from NASA!

They launched a car into space too.
Don't they know there are no roads up there?

10 If Earth was the size of a tennis ball, the Sun would be a ball that is **10m** (33ft) across, approximately 800m (2,600ft) away.

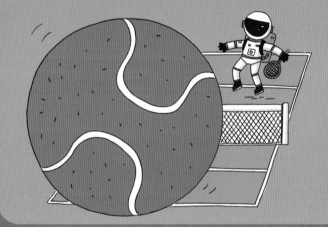

9 If you walked non-stop, it would take around **nine years** to walk to the Moon.

Bear in mind that there are no shoe shops on the way... and no oxygen!

8 Our solar system is moving at about **792,000kmph** (483,000mph).

And, therefore, so are you, sitting there reading this!

7 Venus rotates on its axis so slowly that **one day** on Venus is actually longer than **one year** on Earth!

Some days at school may feel like this too.

★ BRAIN ★ BURSTER

6 The Apollo astronauts' footprints on the Moon may still be there in **one hundred million years**, as there is nothing to disturb them.

THAT'S WHAT YOU THINK!

5

Space has a distinctive **smell**. Astronauts have said that the odour is similar to gunpowder or hot metal.

We blame the Pistol Star!

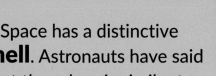

4

When conditions on Jupiter are just right, it literally rains **diamonds**.

Before you get too excited, to collect them you'd have to withstand temperatures of −145°C (−234°F). Chilly!

3

Mars has a mountain, called **Olympus Mons**, which is three times as tall as Mount Everest.

Even cooler, it's a volcano! A giant space volcano!

RECORD BREAKER

2

very **BIG** number

No one can be entirely sure, but scientists estimate that there are around **one septillion** stars in the universe. That's 1,000,000,000,000,000,000,000,000.

Even by very big number standards, that really is a very big number!

1

Driving your family car to Proxima Centauri, our nearest neighbour star after the Sun, at 112kmph (70mph), would take just over **350 billion years**.

WELL, YOU SHOULD HAVE GONE BEFORE WE LEFT!

Fun Space Activities

Use the star charts on pages 12–13 to help you identify **constellations** in the night sky. You could even have races with a friend to see who can find specific constellations first.

Be sure to take a torch and wrap up warm if it's cold outside!

Make **yummy models** of the constellations using marshmallows and cocktail sticks!

Cygnus has 150 stars. You can thank us later!

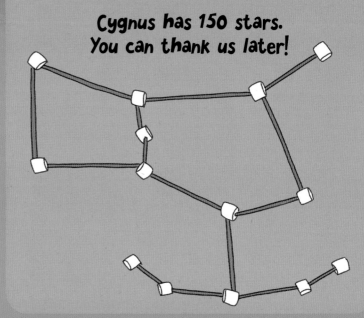

Cut out seven circles of black paper and then use white paint to shade the different phases of the Moon onto them. When you've finished, you can arrange your circles into a giant Moon phases diagram!

Don't forget to add craters and other details!

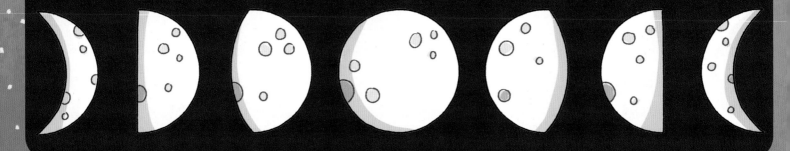

Build a Solar System Mobile

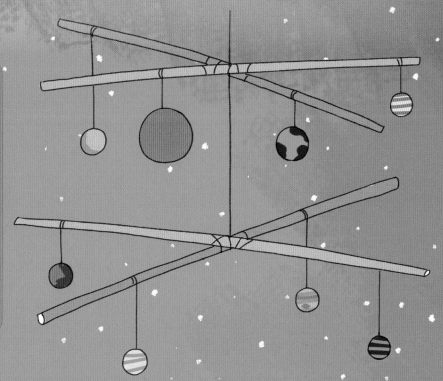

What You'll Need

Old ping-pong balls, plastic balls or other balls that you can paint

Paint and paint brushes

4 garden canes, 40cm in length

String

Thread

Sticky tape

How to Make:

1. Take the balls and **paint them** to look like the planets of the solar system.

2. Take two garden canes and **tape them together to form an 'X' shape**. Do this twice, so you have two garden-cane crosses.

3. Using the string, tie the crosses together so that **one hangs below the other**. Make sure you leave enough string at the top, so you can hang the mobile later. Don't worry if the canes are not perfectly balanced yet.

4. Attach a piece of thread to each of the planets with some tape. Tie a **loose loop** at the end of each thread, so that you can position the planets on the canes.

5. Arrange the planets on the mobile in the order of the solar system (see pages 4–5) and slide them along the canes until the **mobile balances** when hung. Use tape to secure the looped threads on the canes when you're happy with their position. You may need another person to help you!

6. Admire your own **solar system**!

Glossary

Antenna A rod, wire or other device that receives and sends out radio-wave signals.

Asteroids Rocky bodies that orbit the Sun. Most are found between Mars and Jupiter.

Atmosphere The layer of gases surrounding a planet.

Axis An imaginary or real line through the centre of an object, around which the object rotates.

Big Bang A huge explosion, thought to have formed the universe, around 13.8 billion years ago.

Crater A large hole caused by the impact of an object, such as a meteorite.

Eclipse An eclipse happens when one object in space, such as a moon, moves into the shadow of another object so it is obscured.

Equator An imaginary line around the middle of a planet.

Fusion The process that powers stars. Hydrogen atoms (tiny particles) join together (fuse) in a huge burst of energy to form helium atoms.

Hemisphere The northern or southern half of Earth – divided by the equator.

Light year A unit of distance equal to the distance that light travels in a year, which is approximately 9.5 trillion km (6 trillion mi).

Magnetic field The area around something that has magnetic force.

Manned manoeuvring unit A powered backpack device that allows an astronaut to move around the outside of a spacecraft.

Matter The substance, or stuff, that things are made of – whether solid, liquid or gas.

Moon A natural satellite that orbits a planet.

Orbit The curved path of an object in space, such as a moon or spacecraft, around another object, such as a planet or star.

Ozone layer A layer in Earth's atmosphere that contains the gas ozone, which blocks some of the Sun's harmful rays.

Penumbra The area that is partly, but not totally, in shadow during an eclipse.

Phenomenon A fact or event – often one that is remarkable.

Planet A large, round object that orbits a star.

Revolution One complete turn of an object around an axis.

Satellite An object – whether natural or a human-made machine – that orbits a larger object in space.

Satellite mapping systems Satellite systems that use radio waves and image technology to help people find locations.

Shooting star A meteor that looks like a bright light as it streaks across the night sky.

Sumerians People from Sumer, an ancient civilisation, living where modern-day Iraq is currently.

Surface water Water on the surface of a planet, such as lakes, seas or rivers.

Transmission A message or signal that is transmitted (sent or passed on).

Umbra The area that is totally in shadow during an eclipse.

Universe All that exists, including everything in space, such as planets, stars and galaxies.

Unmanned probe A spacecraft without people on board, used to explore space and gather information.

USSR The Union of Soviet Socialist Republic, which existed between 1922 and 1991 and is now Russia.

Weightlessness The feeling of having little or no weight because of a lack of gravity.